The Life & Works of C.S. Lewis

HISTORY BITES ®

Solomon Schmidt

This book is dedicated to my parents, who have continually encouraged and helped me throughout the process of this book.

And to my Uncle Peter Björkman (1953-2017), whose life was greatly impacted by C.S. Lewis. He became a Christian after reading *Mere Christianity*.

And also to Walter Hooper, who has devoted his entire life to advancing C.S. Lewis's legacy. He has been a faithful friend and mentor to me, and I am very grateful for his support.

A Note from the Author

The Life & Works of C.S. Lewis History Bites is a fun and engaging introduction to C.S. Lewis's life and writings. The first seven chapters provide a biographical overview of his life, along with vocabulary and review questions. There is also a glossary at the end of the book for easy reference.

The last nine chapters provide synopses of C.S. Lewis's most popular books, along with a brief overview of their publication history. These sections also include original illustrations by L.B. Dugan, and I am very grateful for her excellent work.

This book serves as a great read aloud and can also be enjoyed by independent readers of all ages.

I really hope you enjoy it.

~Solomon

TABLE OF CONTENTS

The Mourne Mountains in Ireland,
which inspired C.S. Lewis in his creation of Narnia

Solomon at C.S. Lewis's writing desk
in Lewis's home, The Kilns, in Oxford, England

Albert Lewis with his sons, Warren (left) and Clive (right), around 1908

Clive Staples Lewis was born on November 29, 1898, in Belfast, Ireland. His father, Albert Lewis, was a **solicitor** and his mother, Flora, was the daughter of Reverend Thomas Hamilton. Albert met Flora when his family attended St. Mark's Church in Belfast, where Reverend Hamilton was the pastor. Albert fell in love with Flora, but she did not love him at first. However, that eventually changed, and they were married in August of 1894. One year later, on June 16, 1895, their first son, Warren, was born. Three years later, Clive was born.

When Clive was about four years old, he told his family that he wanted to be called "Jacksie." This nickname was eventually shortened to "Jack," and Clive's close friends and family called him that for the rest of his life. Warren and Jack loved spending time together, taking bike rides in the countryside and visiting their friends and family members who lived close by.

In April of 1905, the Lewis family moved from 47 Dundela Avenue to a house called Little Lea, which was in the district of Strandtown in Belfast. There were many rooms in the new house for the brothers to play in and explore. Jack used to spend hours in the "Little End Room" on the third floor, writing stories and drawing pictures. His father had thousands of books, and Jack read many of them. He especially enjoyed reading stories by authors like Lewis Carroll and Beatrix Potter.

During this time, Warren and Jack created an imaginary land together, called Boxen, which was made up of two separate worlds: India (Warren's world) and Animal-Land (Jack's world). One of the characters they created was a talking frog named Lord Big.

Sadly, Jack's happy childhood was about to change. On August 23, 1908, when he was only nine years old, his mother, Flora Lewis, died of cancer. Jack was very sad and lonely because his mother was not there to comfort him anymore. Jack's father, Albert Lewis, was deeply distressed, and he was never very close to his sons after his wife's death.

2

Soon after his mother's death, Jack was separated from his father and brother when he was sent to England to become a student at Wynyard School in Hertfordshire. It was very hard for him to live there because the **headmaster**, Robert Capron, was mean to the boys and sometimes beat them. In June of 1910, Jack left the school, and later that fall, he attended Campbell College in Belfast, Ireland. He was very happy there and especially enjoyed his English class, which was taught by Lewis Alden.

In January of 1911, Jack moved back to England to attend Cherbourg School in Malvern. His brother, Warren, was attending school close by at Malvern College, and they were able to see each other more often. While he was at Cherbourg, Jack stopped believing in Christianity, which was the religion his parents had taught him. He had become very angry with God after his mother's death. Also, a teacher at Cherbourg School named Miss Cowie had led him away from the Christian faith with her anti-Christian beliefs.

After living at Cherbourg School for two years, Jack became a student at Malvern College in September of 1913. He found it difficult to live there because of a group of older boys known as the "Bloods." Some of them used to bully Jack because he was younger and new to the school. Although Warren had been happy at Malvern, Jack wanted to leave.

In April of 1914, while on a holiday at home, Jack visited a young man named Arthur Greeves, who was sick at the time. The Greeves were friends of the Lewis family, and Jack and

Arthur became close friends because of their shared love of Old Norse literature. Throughout the rest of Jack's life, the two friends wrote hundreds of letters to each other, talking about their families, religion, and many other things.

Little Lea, the Lewis family home in Belfast, Ireland

Malvern College in Malvern, England

REVIEW BITES

VOCABULARY

Solicitor – a type of lawyer in Great Britain who represents people in the lower courts

District – an area of land in a city

Headmaster – the person in charge of a private school

Literature – a collection of writings that have great value and importance

FUN FACT

Warren and Jack had a lot of fun times together when they were young, but sometimes they got into trouble. Their nurse, Lizzie Endicott, would tell them that she was going to smack their little "piggiebottoms" if they did not stop misbehaving. Because of this, the Lewis brothers gave themselves the nicknames "Archpiggiebotham" (for Warren) and "Smallpiggiebotham" (for Jack).

REVIEW QUESTIONS

1. When and where was C.S. Lewis born?

2. Who was Jack's brother?

3. How old was Jack when his mother died?

Wartime
(1914-1918)

Trenches in World War I

In June of 1914, Jack's father, Albert, removed him from Malvern College. Jack spent that summer at home in Belfast. In September, he traveled to Great Bookham in Surrey, England, to live with and be **tutored** by a man named William T. Kirkpatrick. Mr. Kirkpatrick had also taught Jack's father and his brother, Warren, who was training to be a soldier at the Royal Military College in Sandhurst.

Soon after Jack moved in with Mr. Kirkpatrick and his wife, World War I began. Germany, Austria-Hungary, and their allies (the Central Powers) fought against Great Britain, France, and their allies. In November of 1914, Warren Lewis left England to fight the Germans in France. Jack, who was too young to join the army, continued his studies with Mr. Kirkpatrick.

William Kirkpatrick was a very **logical** man, and he was also an atheist, which is someone who does not believe in the existence of God. He taught Jack to think critically about certain issues and determine if they were right or wrong. Jack also studied the writings of a man named Homer, who lived during ancient times and wrote *The Iliad* and *The Odyssey*. He learned how to translate Greek words into English and was eventually able to read entire books in Greek.

One day, on March 4, 1916, Jack was at a railroad station waiting for his train to come in when he saw a bookstall (a newsstand where magazines and books are sold). He bought a fantasy novel called *Phantastes* by a Christian author named George MacDonald. He later said that it was very influential in helping to develop his imagination.

In December of 1916, Jack went to Oxford, England, because he wanted to study at Oxford University, which is made up of thirty-nine separate colleges. He received a **scholarship** to University College, but in order to be accepted into Oxford University, he had to pass a test called Responsions. Jack took the test in March of 1917 but did not pass the math portion. However, he was still allowed to begin studying at University College so that he could join the Oxford University Officers' Training Corps. Once he completed the officers' training, Jack could become an officer in the British Army and fight in World War I. So, from

April to June of 1917, he studied at University College and trained for the military at Keble College (another one of Oxford University's thirty-nine colleges).

While he was at Keble College, Jack met and became friends with a young man named Edward "Paddy" Moore, who was also training to fight in the war. Jack met Paddy's mother, Janie, and his younger sister, Maureen, and he became very close with the Moore family.

On September 26, 1917, Jack became an officer in the British Army and was later assigned to the Somerset Light Infantry, which was going to be stationed in France. Before he left for France, he spent time with the Moore family in Oxford and also visited his father in Belfast. Jack and Paddy made an agreement that if one of them was killed during the war, the other man would take care of his family.

In November of 1917, Jack sailed to France with his **regiment**, and soon after arriving, he was fighting in the trenches against the Germans. The experience of war greatly impacted Jack's thoughts about life and God. He wrote some poetry during this time that later became part of his first book, *Spirits in Bondage*.

In February of 1918, Jack got sick with a mysterious disease called "trench fever." He spent one month in the hospital and then returned to the trenches. He fought in the Battle of Arras, and on April 15, 1918, he was wounded by a shell that exploded near him on Mont-Bernanchon. Because of his serious injuries, he was sent back to England one month later and never returned to France. Jack spent time in a hospital in London to recover, and in December of 1918, he was demobilized from the British Army.

Sadly, Jack's friend Edward "Paddy" Moore had been killed in March of 1918 while fighting against the Germans. Jack was very sad and knew that it was his duty to honor the promise he had made to his friend and look after Paddy's mother and sister.

Royal Military College in Sandhurst, England, around 1895

Author George MacDonald

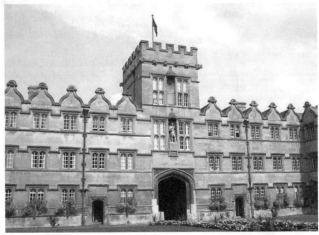

University College, Oxford University

VOCABULARY

Tutored – taught privately about a particular subject

Logical – thinking through something clearly

Scholarship – a gift of money to attend a college or university

Regiment – a unit of soldiers in the military that is usually made up of two battalions

Demobilized – released from the military

FUN FACT

C.S. Lewis always struggled with math. Even when he got older, he could never pass a basic Algebra test.

REVIEW QUESTIONS

1. Who was Jack's tutor in Great Bookham, Surrey, England?

2. To what Oxford University college did Jack receive a scholarship?

3. During what battle in World War I was Jack wounded?

C.S. Lewis in 1919

In January of 1919, Jack returned to University College to take a course called "Honour Mods," in which he studied Greek and Latin literature.

On March 20, 1919, Jack's first book, called *Spirits in Bondage*, was published. It was a collection of poems he had written over the years and included many of his hateful feelings toward God. His angry feelings started after his mother's death and got worse because of the things he had learned from his childhood teacher, Miss Cowie, and the terrible things he had seen while fighting in World War I.

Jack's close friends, Janie and Maureen Moore (Paddy's mother and sister), lived close to Oxford University in a village called Headington. Jack would work at University College in the morning and visit the Moores in the afternoon. During this time in his life, Jack's father, Albert, helped to support him **financially**, and Jack used some of the money to help provide for the Moore family.

Around this same time, in 1919, Jack met and became good friends with a man named Owen Barfield, who was studying at Wadham College, which was part of Oxford University. Owen was a Christian, and the two men used to debate about religion and history. Jack referred to their debates as the "Great War." Despite their disagreements, they enjoyed spending time together and taking walks around Oxford with their friend Cecil Harwood.

In March of 1920, Jack passed his "Honour Mods" tests with **flying colors**. These exams are given after someone finishes the first year of college at Oxford University. Jack then began a program called "Greats," in which he studied **philosophy** and ancient history. While he was in this new program, in June of 1921, he moved from his room at University College to live with the Moores in Headington. He continued with his studies and also regularly did chores around the house for Mrs. Moore. (He continued to do so for as long as they lived together.)

In June of 1922, Jack passed the exams for "Greats," and in the fall, he began a course of study in English language and literature. He took the final exams in June of 1923 and received First Class Honors, which is the highest grade a student at Oxford University can achieve. He tried to get a **fellowship** to one of the Oxford Colleges but was unsuccessful. A fellow is a member of a college who studies and teaches about a particular subject.

In May of 1924, Jack agreed to fill in for the position of philosophy tutor at University College for E.F. Carritt, who was spending the next **academic year** in America. In October of 1924, Jack gave his first lecture, and he also began tutoring several young men. Throughout the year, he sometimes visited his father, Albert, in Belfast, Ireland.

In May of 1925, Mr. Lewis was elected to a Fellowship of English Language and Literature at Magdalen College at Oxford University. He moved there in October of that same year, began lecturing and tutoring, and held this position for almost thirty years.

On May 11, 1926, Mr. Lewis met a man named John Ronald Revel (J.R.R.) Tolkien, the future author of *The Hobbit* and *The Lord of the Rings*. They became good friends, spent a lot of time together, and shared stories and ideas with each other. In fact, Mr. Tolkien once said that without Mr. Lewis encouraging him to keep writing, he would have never finished *The Lord of the Rings*.

On September 20, 1926, Mr. Lewis's second book, called *Dymer*, was published. It was a long poem that he had been writing on and off since 1916.

During this same time, Mr. Lewis's brother, Warren, was an officer in the British Army, and because of this, the two of them did not get to see each other very much. In April of 1927,

Warren sailed from England to Shanghai, China, and served there with the Royal Army Service Corps for three years.

Meanwhile, their father's health was getting worse. In August of 1929, Mr. Lewis visited his father in Belfast, and one month later, the doctors discovered that he had cancer. On September 25, 1929, Albert Lewis died in Belfast, Ireland. Mr. Lewis was very sorry that he had not been as kind and loving to his father as he knew he should have been. This was something he felt guilty about for the rest of his life.

J.R.R. Tolkien

City hall in Belfast, Ireland, in 1911

Magdalen College, Oxford University

VOCABULARY

Financially – having to do with money

Flying colors – passing a test easily with a very good grade

Philosophy – the study of knowledge

Fellowship – the rank of a fellow at a college

Academic year – this was the time from October to early July while C.S. Lewis was at Oxford University

FUN FACT

C.S. Lewis wrote poetry his whole life. Some of his poems were published during his lifetime, but many of them were collected after his death and published in two books, called *Poems* and *Narrative Poems*. In 2013, a stone with his name on it was placed in Poets' Corner in Westminster Abbey in London, England.

REVIEW QUESTIONS

1. What was Mr. Lewis's first book called?

2. To what Oxford College did
Mr. Lewis receive a fellowship?

3. Whom did Mr. Lewis meet in 1926?
(Hint: he later became a famous author)

1. *Spirits in Bondage* 2. Magdalen College
3. J.R.R. Tolkien.

Conversion and the Inklings
(1929-1938)

The Kilns in Oxford, England

Near the end of 1929, Mr. Lewis and the Moores were looking for a house to live in permanently. In April of 1930, Warren came home from China and helped Mr. Lewis sell their family home, called Little Lea, in Ireland. Then, in July of 1930, the Lewis brothers and Mrs. Moore put their money together to buy a home in Headington, Oxford, called The Kilns. The Kilns was a large house surrounded by a lot of land, trees, and also a pond, which the Lewis brothers swam in many times. Throughout the years he lived there, Mr. Lewis hired housemaids and also a **handyman** named Fred Paxford. Mr. Paxford was a good friend of the Lewis and Moore families for many years. Interestingly, because of Mr. Paxford's gloomy outlook on life, he eventually became Mr. Lewis's model for the despairing character Puddleglum in *The Silver Chair.*

During this time, Mr. Lewis's thoughts about God were greatly changing. After many years of struggling to believe in God, in 1929, Mr. Lewis became a **theist**. He later called himself the "most...**reluctant** convert in all England." However, he still did not believe in Christianity.

On September 19, 1931, Mr. Lewis had dinner at Magdalen College with J.R.R. Tolkien and their friend Hugo Dyson. Later that night, while on Addison's Walk at Magdalen College, Mr. Tolkien told Mr. Lewis that the Gospel of Jesus Christ was not just another myth, but was truth grounded in historical fact. Soon after this important conversation, Mr. Lewis came to believe that Jesus Christ is God. He then joined the Church of England and became an Anglican.

In August of 1932, Mr. Lewis wrote a story about his conversion to Christianity, called *The Pilgrim's Regress.* It was published in 1933, and it tells the story of a pilgrim named John, who journeys on a road and is searching for truth. Along the way, he meets many people who try to lead him away from the path. However, when he reaches the end of the road, John finally realizes that Christianity is the truth he had been searching for all along.

Near the end of 1932, Mr. Lewis's brother, Warren, retired from the British Army. In 1933, the group called the Inklings was formed, and it included the Lewis brothers, Mr. Tolkien, and some of their friends. They met on Tuesday mornings at a **pub** called The Eagle and Child in Oxford and on Thursday nights at Magdalen College. They talked about many subjects and shared their writings with each other. The regular Inklings meetings continued until 1949. After this, the group met once a week on Mondays or Tuesdays until Mr. Lewis's death in 1963.

In February of 1936, Mr. Lewis read a book called *The Place of the Lion* by Charles Williams. He enjoyed it so much that he wrote a fan letter to Mr. Williams, who worked for the Oxford University Press in London at the time. The two men became good friends, and in 1939, Mr. Williams moved to Oxford and became an important member of the Inklings. Sadly, Mr. Williams died unexpectedly in 1945 at the age of fifty-eight. The members of the Inklings were very sad to have lost their friend.

On May 21, 1936, Mr. Lewis's book *The Allegory of Love* was published. It was a study of love and poetry from medieval times and was very well received by many people.

Mr. Lewis continued to write. He and Mr. Tolkien met and agreed that there were not enough books of the kind they wanted to read. So, they decided to write some themselves. Soon after, Mr. Lewis began writing *Out of the Silent Planet*, which is the first book in what became *The Space Trilogy*. It was published in 1938, and it was the story of a man named Dr. Elwin Ranson, who has adventures in space and journeys to the planet Malacandra (Mars). The second book in *The Space Trilogy*, *Perelandra*, was published in 1943, and it was about Dr. Ransom's journey to the planet Perelandra (Venus). The people

Dr. Ransom meets on Malacandra and Perelandra are unfallen, which means that they have not sinned (done wrong).

The third and final book, *That Hideous Strength*, was published in 1945. In this story, Dr. Ransom stays on Earth and helps a couple named Jane and Mark Studdock face an evil organization called N.I.C.E. In all three books, Mr. Lewis's goal was to write stories about space from a Christian point of view, and because of this, they are full of theology (teachings about God). *The Space Trilogy* has become one of C.S. Lewis's most popular writings.

The Eagle and Child pub

Addison's Walk, Magdalen College

VOCABULARY

Handyman – a person who is hired to fix things around a house

Theist – someone who believes in the existence of God

Reluctant – hesitant to make a decision

Regress – going back to something

Pub – a bar or tavern that serves food and drinks

FUN FACT

C.S. Lewis had many pets at The Kilns. One of them was a dog named Mr. Papworth, who was a terrier. For some reason, Mr. Papworth would never eat his food when people were watching him. When C.S. Lewis took him for walks, he would throw food behind his back so that the dog could eat without anyone watching.

REVIEW QUESTIONS

1. What was the name of the house that the Lewis and Moore families bought in 1930?

2. When and where did Mr. Lewis have an important conversation with J.R.R. Tolkien about Christianity?

3. What book did Mr. Lewis publish in 1938 that was the first part of *The Space Trilogy?*

C.S. Lewis in his study at Magdalen College in 1947

In 1939, World War II began. The Axis (Germany, Italy, Japan, and their allies) were fighting against the Allies (Great Britain, France, and their allies). Since he was part of the **army reserve**, Warren Lewis had to go to war to help England fight against the Axis. He became a major in the British Army, and after one year of fighting in the war, he returned home to Oxford, where he lived for the rest of his life.

Because of his work at Oxford University, C.S. Lewis was allowed to remain in England and continue teaching. In October of 1940, he published his first nonfiction book that defended Christianity. It was called *The Problem of Pain* and quickly became very popular. Earlier that year, Mr. Lewis had an idea for a book that was later called *The Screwtape Letters*. There are thirty-one letters in this book, and from May to November of 1941, they were published one at a time each week in a magazine called *The Guardian*. In February of 1942, *The Screwtape Letters* was published in book form. It sold very well in England and America and helped to make Mr. Lewis famous among Christian readers.

Even though he did not fight, Mr. Lewis served his country during World War II. He traveled throughout Great Britain to teach about Christianity and other subjects to members of the Royal Air Force (RAF). He and Mrs. Moore also took in three English **refugee** schoolgirls at The Kilns, so they would be safe from attacks by the Nazi German air force. One of the girls was Jill Flewett, who later became the wife of Clement Freud, Sigmund Freud's grandson. (You can learn about Sigmund Freud in my fifth book, *In/Famous People History Bites Volume 2*.) Some people believe that Jill Flewett was the inspiration for the character Lucy Pevensie in *The Chronicles of Narnia*.

In February of 1941, Dr. James Welch, who worked for the British Broadcasting Corporation (BBC), invited Mr. Lewis to give a series of talks on the radio about Christianity. Mr. Lewis agreed, and his first series of talks **aired** on the radio in August and September of 1941. He went on to give three more series of talks about Christianity, which were heard by millions of people in Great Britain. This greatly increased his popularity as a Christian **apologist**. Eventually, Mr. Lewis expanded and compiled all four series of talks into a book called *Mere Christianity*, which was published in 1952 and has sold millions of copies.

Mr. Lewis continued to write and teach. On June 8, 1941, he preached a now-famous sermon called "The Weight of Glory" at the University Church of St. Mary the Virgin in Oxford. In 1944, his book *The Abolition of Man* was published, and it was based on three lectures he had given in 1943 at the University of Durham in England. In this book, Mr. Lewis defended the idea that right and wrong exist and that people cannot make up their own ideas about morality.

In January of 1946, Mr. Lewis published another book, called *The Great Divorce*, which is about a fictional (make-believe) bus ride from Hell to Heaven. One year later, in 1947, he published the book *Miracles*, and in it, he defended the teaching that God can and does perform miracles.

In February of 1948, a woman named Elizabeth Anscombe argued against something that Mr. Lewis had written in Chapter 3 of *Miracles* about a belief called naturalism. She brought up her disagreement at a meeting of the Socratic Club, which met regularly at Oxford University to discuss different parts of the Christian religion. Mr. Lewis was the president of the club, and he regularly defeated people in debates. Some members of the club were shocked that Ms. Anscombe had made her comments against *Miracles* in public with Mr. Lewis sitting right there listening. Surprisingly, though, Mr. Lewis came to agree with her points and later revised some parts of Chapter 3 in *Miracles* for a new edition of the book. This whole event is known as the "Lewis-Anscombe Debate" and has interested many scholars since.

Air raid shelter that C.S. Lewis built at The Kilns during World War II

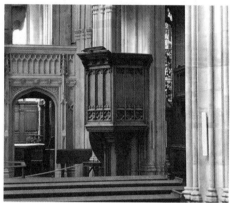

Pulpit from which C.S. Lewis delivered his sermon "The Weight of Glory"

University Church of St. Mary the Virgin in Oxford, England

VOCABULARY

Army reserve – a group of soldiers ready to fight when called to active duty

Refugee – a person who has to leave his/her home in order to escape danger

Aired – played or broadcast on television or radio

Apologist – someone who defends his/her religion through books and speeches

FUN FACT

On September 8, 1947, a drawing of C.S. Lewis appeared on the cover of *Time* magazine because of his popularity in England and America.

REVIEW QUESTIONS

1. What book did Mr. Lewis publish in 1942?

2. On what radio station did Mr. Lewis give four series of talks about Christianity?

3. Who disagreed with something written in Chapter 3 of Mr. Lewis's book *Miracles?*

Narnia and Cambridge
(1949-1954)

C.S. Lewis at Magdalen College, Oxford University, in 1950

Mr. Lewis once said that when he was sixteen years old, a picture of a faun in a snowy wood popped into his head. (In Greek mythology, a faun is a half-man, half-goat creature.) Mr. Lewis later decided to write a story around this faun. More pictures and ideas came to him, and in 1949, he wrote *The Lion, the Witch and the Wardrobe*, which is a children's fictional story with Christian messages woven throughout. Mr. Lewis received inspiration from an English author named Edith Nesbit (1858-1924), who also wrote children's stories.

Mr. Lewis gave the **manuscript** of *The Lion, the Witch and the Wardrobe* to his friend Roger Lancelyn Green, who greatly enjoyed it and encouraged him to publish it. By the end of 1949, Mr. Lewis had finished writing the second Narnia story, called *Prince Caspian: The Return to Narnia.* Amazingly, just a couple months later, in February of 1950, he finished writing the third book in the series, which was called *The Voyage of the Dawn Treader.*

By the time *The Lion, the Witch and the Wardrobe* was published in October of 1950, Mr. Lewis had completed another Narnia story: *The Horse and His Boy.* When he finished writing the manuscript of each book, he would give it to Mr. Green for his thoughts and advice. In March of 1951, Mr. Green read the manuscript of *The Silver Chair,* which was eventually published in 1953.

After *The Silver Chair,* Mr. Lewis wrote two more Narnia tales: *The Last Battle* and *The Magician's Nephew.* All seven books together make up *The Chronicles of Narnia* series and have become some of the most beloved and best-selling children's books of all time. Mr. Lewis hired an artist named Pauline Baynes to illustrate the entire series.

Sadly, during the time he was writing *The Chronicles of Narnia,* on January 17, 1951, Mrs. Moore died at the age of seventy-eight. For many years, she had been like a mother to Mr. Lewis, even though she took advantage of his helpful personality many times and had him do a lot of work around The Kilns.

In August of 1952, a woman named Helen Joy Davidman Gresham sailed to England to meet Mr. Lewis. Mrs. Gresham lived in New York with her husband, William, and two sons, David and Douglas. She was a Christian and had been **corresponding** with Mr. Lewis for two years. They first met at the Eastgate Hotel in Oxford, and Mr. Lewis enjoyed her company. She had a great knowledge of literature and was sometimes very **blunt**. Unfortunately, her husband, William, had been unfaithful to her and wanted to marry someone else. When Joy returned home to New York, she and William decided to get a divorce. Then, in November of 1953, Joy and her sons, David and Douglas, moved to London, England. Mr. Lewis visited them regularly and helped pay for the boys' schooling.

In June of 1954, Mr. Lewis accepted a teaching position at Cambridge University in England. He became the Professor of Medieval and Renaissance English at Magdalene College (not to be confused with Magdalen College at Oxford University). Mr. Lewis lived at Cambridge during the week and came home to Oxford on weekends. He really enjoyed his time at Magdalene College and believed that moving there was one of the best decisions of his career.

In September of 1954, Mr. Lewis published a book called *English Literature in the Sixteenth Century, Excluding Drama*. In it, he overviewed the writings of many authors from the 1500s, such as David Lyndsay and Thomas More. This book helped to make Mr. Lewis a well-known **literary critic**.

The Eastgate Hotel, where C.S. Lewis first met Joy Davidman

Magdalene College, Cambridge University

REVIEW BITES

VOCABULARY

Manuscript – a copy of a book that is written by hand and has not been published yet

Corresponding – writing back and forth

Blunt – to the point or very direct

Literary critic – someone who studies and writes about works of literature

FUN FACT

In 1952, C.S. Lewis got a call from the Court Stairs Hotel in Kent, England, asking when he was going to pay his "wife's" bill. Shocked, he discovered that a woman named Mrs. Hooker had claimed to be his wife and had put all of her hotel bills on his account. Later that same year, he traveled to Canterbury, England, to testify against her in court. She was found guilty and was sent to jail.

REVIEW QUESTIONS

1. What was the first book Mr. Lewis wrote in *The Chronicles of Narnia* series?

2. Who sailed to England in August of 1952 to meet Mr. Lewis?

3. In 1954, what position did Mr. Lewis accept at Cambridge University?

1. *The Lion, the Witch and the Wardrobe*
2. Helen Joy Davidman Gresham
3. Professor of Medieval and Renaissance English

7 Marriage and Last Years (1955-1963)

C.S. Lewis at his writing desk in 1963
(Used by permission of Walter Hooper)

Solomon at C.S. Lewis's
writing desk in 2019

In September of 1955, Mr. Lewis's **autobiography**, *Surprised by Joy*, was published. In this book, he wrote about his early life and how he came to believe in Christianity.

Later that same year, the British Home Office would not renew Joy Davidman's **visa**, and because of this, she was going to have to leave England. So, Mr. Lewis agreed to marry her at a **registry office** so that she could become a British citizen and remain in the country. He was not in love with her (yet), but on April 23, 1956, they were married at the Oxford Registry Office.

In the beginning of their marriage, Joy Davidman lived separately from Mr. Lewis. Then, on October 18, 1956, she collapsed in her home and was rushed to the hospital. The doctors told her that she had cancer. After learning this sad news, Mr. Lewis realized that he loved Joy, and he could not bear the thought of living life without her. They wanted to have a Christian marriage ceremony before she died.

So, on March 21, 1957, C.S. Lewis and Joy Davidman were married by the Reverend Peter Bide in the Wingfield-Morris Hospital (at her bedside). Mr. Lewis's brother, Warren, was there to witness the ceremony.

Then something amazing happened. Just two months later, in May of 1957, Mrs. Lewis's doctors discovered that her cancer was gone! Mr. Lewis believed it was a miracle. Mrs. Lewis came home to The Kilns, and after spending some time recovering there, she was able to move around the house without the help of a nurse. She set to work cleaning up The Kilns and giving it a "woman's touch." Mr. and Mrs. Lewis enjoyed their new life together and loved each other very much.

While all of these events were taking place, Mr. Lewis found time to continue writing. In September of 1956, he published a fictional book called *Till We Have Faces*, which he believed was one of his best books. In 1958, he published *Reflections on the Psalms*, which was a study of the Book of Psalms from the Bible. That same year, Mr. Lewis recorded a series of talks about love for the Episcopal Radio-TV Foundation. These talks later became the **basis** for his book *The Four Loves*, which was published in March of 1960.

In October of 1959, Mrs. Lewis went to the hospital for a routine check-up, and the doctors discovered that her cancer had returned. Mr. Lewis was very sad, and he wanted to bless his wife one more time before she died. So, in April of 1960, he took her to the place she had always dreamed of visiting: Greece. Mr. and Mrs. Lewis journeyed around the country for almost two weeks with their friends Roger Lancelyn Green and his wife, June.

On July 13, 1960, just a few months after they had returned home from Greece, Joy Lewis died at the Radcliffe Infirmary (hospital) in Oxford. Mr. Lewis felt very lonely, depressed, and afraid after his wife's death. In spite of his grief, he decided to adopt and take care of her sons, David and Douglas.

In September of 1961, Mr. Lewis published *A Grief Observed*, in which he described his deep sadness after losing his wife. At first, Mr. Lewis was angry at God because of Joy's death. However, his faith eventually became stronger when he realized that God had a purpose in Joy's death, even though it was hard for him to understand at times.

During most of the academic year of 1961–1962, Mr. Lewis could not teach at Cambridge University because of health problems. In June of 1963, a young American named Walter Hooper, who admired Mr. Lewis's works, came to England to meet Mr. Lewis. During Mr. Hooper's time in Oxford, Mr. Lewis asked him to be his secretary since it was becoming harder for him to write. Mr. Hooper agreed, and they met regularly at The Kilns and attended services together at Holy Trinity Church in Oxford.

On July 15, 1963, Mr. Lewis had to go to the Acland Nursing Home because of his failing health. Just one day later, he had a heart attack but soon recovered and was able to return home to The Kilns. In August of 1963, Walter Hooper went home to the United States to finish some business, but he planned to return to England in 1964 to work full time as Mr. Lewis's secretary. That same month, Mr. Lewis resigned from his position at Cambridge University.

Sadly, Mr. Hooper never got the chance to work for Mr. Lewis again. On November 22, 1963, C.S. Lewis died of kidney failure at The Kilns in the arms of his brother, Warren. (Interestingly, it was the same day U.S. President John F. Kennedy was shot and killed in Dallas, Texas.)

Since his death, C.S. Lewis has become one of the most popular and beloved authors of all time. His books have sold hundreds of millions of copies around the world and have been translated into dozens of languages. In addition to his books, three very successful films have been made based on *The Lion, the Witch and the Wardrobe, Prince Caspian,* and *The Voyage of the Dawn Treader.*

C.S. Lewis and Walter Hooper in 1963
(Used by permission of Walter Hooper)

Solomon and Walter Hooper in 2019
at The Trout Inn, Oxford, England

REVIEW BITES

VOCABULARY

Autobiography – a book that someone writes about his/her own life

Visa – permission from the government to enter and live in a country for a limited time

Registry office – a place in Great Britain where people get married and where birth and death records are kept

Basis – the primary idea behind a book

FUN FACT

From 1959-1962, C.S. Lewis was a member of the Commission to Revise the Psalter. This group met every few months, and their goal was to correct some mistakes in the Psalter, which was a book used during Anglican church services. While he was part of this group, C.S. Lewis became friends with another author named T.S. Eliot, who wrote many famous poems, including "The Waste Land" (1922).

REVIEW QUESTIONS

1. Whom did Mr. Lewis marry in 1956?

2. Where did Mr. Lewis take his wife before she died?

3. When and where did C.S. Lewis die?

1. Joy Davidman 2. Greece
3. November 22, 1963, at his home,
The Kilns, in Oxford, England

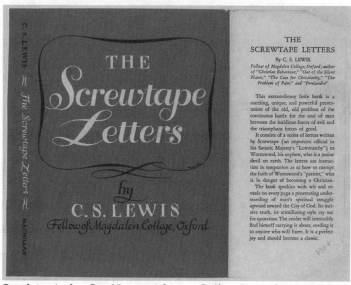

Dust jacket of a 1944 edition of The Screwtape Letters

On Sunday, July 21, 1940, while attending services at Holy Trinity Church, C.S. Lewis got the idea for what eventually became *The Screwtape Letters*. Although historians are not exactly sure how long it took him to write it, it is likely that Mr. Lewis completed the book by the end of 1940. This book includes thirty-one letters, and from May to November of 1941, they were published individually each week in a magazine called *The Guardian*. In 1942, the letters were published together in book form by Geoffrey Bles, who was a British publisher.

The Screwtape Letters sold many copies and made Mr. Lewis very popular among Christian readers. In 1959, he published a short story called "Screwtape Proposes a Toast," and it was later included at the end of *The Screwtape Letters*. Here is a brief synopsis of the book:

Screwtape is an older devil who is writing letters from Hell to his nephew, Wormwood, a junior devil. He gives Wormwood advice on the best way to tempt people to sin (do wrong things). Wormwood is in charge of the temptation of a young man, whom Screwtape calls the "patient." All of Screwtape's letters are written from an evil perspective. Because of this, the Christian God is referred to as "the Enemy," and the "advice" that Screwtape gives to Wormwood is meant to be a warning to readers about how to guard against temptation.

Wormwood's "patient" becomes a Christian, and Screwtape writes to Wormwood about how to tempt the young man to sin against others, especially against his difficult mother. Screwtape explains to him that he can take things "the Enemy" (God) has created and use them to tempt the "patient." Screwtape also tells Wormwood that he should make sure the "patient" never realizes that a devil is there tempting him to sin. However, one day, the "patient" understands what Wormwood is trying to do to him, and because of this, he becomes a stronger Christian. Screwtape becomes very angry with Wormwood, and in the last letter, he tells Wormwood that he is going to face punishment for his failure to tempt the "patient" properly.

At the end of the book, in the section called "Screwtape Proposes a Toast," there is a dinner being given at the Tempters' Training College in Hell. During this dinner, Screwtape gives a speech, in which he praises modern English education because of its anti-Christian teachings. At the end of his speech, Screwtape proposes a toast to the devils in the audience.

The sanctuary of Holy Trinity Church, where C.S. Lewis first got the idea for The Screwtape Letters

Solomon in front of Holy Trinity Church in Oxford, England, in 2019

Mere Christianity: A Synopsis (1952)

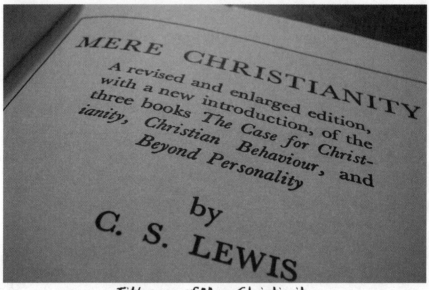

Title page of Mere Christianity

In 1941, C.S. Lewis was asked to give a series of radio talks about Christianity for the British Broadcasting Corporation (BBC). He went on to give three more series of talks over the next few years (see Chapter 5: "The Christian Apologist"). The first series was called "Right and Wrong: A Clue to the Meaning of the Universe." It included five talks, which aired once a week from August 6, 1941 – September 6, 1941. The second series was called "What Christians Believe," and it also included five radio talks, which aired once a week from January 11, 1942 – February 15, 1942. That same year, these first two series of talks were published together in a book called *Broadcast Talks*.

The third series of talks Mr. Lewis gave for the BBC was called "Christian Behaviour" (note: in Great Britain, "behavior" is spelled differently). This series included eight radio talks, which aired once a week from September 20, 1942 – November 8, 1942. In 1943, this series was published as a book called *Christian Behaviour*. Mr. Lewis's fourth radio series was called "Beyond Personality," and it included seven talks, which aired once a week from February 22, 1944 – April 4, 1944. That same year, this series was published as a book called *Beyond Personality: The Christian Idea of God*.

Several years later, Mr. Lewis compiled and expanded his four series of radio talks into one book, called *Mere Christianity*, which was published in 1952 by Geoffrey Bles. Here is a brief synopsis of it:

Mere Christianity is an overview of some of the most important teachings about Christianity. Book 1 is titled "Right and Wrong as a Clue to the Meaning of the Universe." This section defends the idea that right and wrong exist and that people feel badly when they break the moral law. This argument leads into Book 2, which is entitled "What Christians Believe." This section teaches that there is a God behind the moral law and that He gives people a conscience, which helps them understand right and wrong. Book 2 also explains that if people believe Jesus Christ's death was a sacrifice for their sins, then they are made right with God.

Book 3, which is entitled "Christian Behaviour," is about how Christians are supposed to think and act. Three of the chapters focus on forgiveness, hope, and faith.

The last part of *Mere Christianity* is Book 4, which is called "Beyond Personality: Or First Steps in the Doctrine of the Trinity." This section overviews several important points of theology, such as the Trinity, which is the Christian belief that God exists as three persons in One: the Father, the Son, and the Holy Spirit. The final chapter in Book 4 is called "The New Men," and it teaches that people should not trust in themselves, but should put their trust in Christ.

My late Uncle Peter Björkman, who became a Christian after reading Mere Christianity

BBC Broadcasting House, where C.S. Lewis gave
his four series of radio talks on Christianity

10 The Magician's Nephew: A Synopsis (1955)

Aslan Creating the World of Narnia *by L.B. Dugan*

C.S. Lewis finished writing *The Magician's Nephew* by February of 1954. It was the last book written in *The Chronicles of Narnia* series but is the first book in chronological order. Because of this, *The Magician's Nephew* is often listed as the first Narnia story. Mr. Lewis dedicated this book to the Kilmer Family of Washington, D.C., with whom he had written several letters (most of these can be found in a book called *C.S. Lewis: Letters to Children*). *The Magician's Nephew* was published in 1955 by Geoffrey Bles. Here is a brief synopsis of it:

Digory Kirke lives in London with his mother, who is very sick, and his mean uncle, Andrew Ketterley, who practices magic. Digory becomes friends with a girl next door named Polly Plummer.

One day, the two children wander into Uncle Andrew's study, where he keeps his collection of magic rings. Digory and Polly accidentally use these rings to enter into an ancient and ruined world called Charn. While they are wandering through Charn, Digory mistakenly awakens Queen Jadis, who has been under a deep spell. Digory and Polly try to escape from Jadis's clutches, but when they use the rings to return to London, they discover that the evil queen has come with them.

Digory and Polly realize that they need to transport Queen Jadis back to Charn immediately. However, they accidentally take Uncle Andrew and a man named Frank and his horse, Strawberry, with them. (Frank's wife, Helen, is magically brought to them later in the story.)

Unexpectedly, instead of bringing them to Charn, the magic rings bring them to the land of Narnia at the time it is being created. Aslan, a great talking lion, is singing the world into existence. He creates many animals, some of which are given the ability to speak.

Queen Jadis runs away, and Aslan tells Digory to bring back an apple from a garden in the Western Wild. Aslan wants to use a seed from this apple to grow a tree that will be used to protect the Narnians from Jadis. To help Digory reach the garden quickly, Aslan gives wings to Strawberry, the horse, and changes his name to Fledge.

Digory and Polly travel to the garden on the back of Fledge, who flies over the newly created world of Narnia. When Digory enters the garden, he finds Queen Jadis. She has eaten one of the magic apples, and she tempts Digory to take one for his own benefit and not for Aslan. Digory resists the temptation and brings an apple back to Aslan. Aslan rewards Digory for his obedience by letting him take another magic apple back to his sick mother in London in order to make her well. Before Digory and Polly leave Narnia, they attend a ceremony in which Frank and his wife, Helen, are crowned the first King and Queen of Narnia.

Digory, Polly, and Uncle Andrew return to London. Digory gives the magic apple to his mother, and she is healed of her sickness. A tree eventually grows from a seed of this apple. Many years later, Digory becomes a professor, and he uses the wood of this tree to build a wardrobe (tall clothing cabinet) for his country home.

Digory, Polly, and Fledge Fly to the Garden *by L.B. Dugan*

The White Witch in Her Sleigh *by L.B. Dugan*

The story of *The Lion, the Witch and the Wardrobe* came about as a result of images that popped into C.S. Lewis's head, such as a faun in a snowy wood and a great lion (see Chapter 6: "Narnia and Cambridge"). He wrote the story in early 1949, and it was the first book written in *The Chronicles of Narnia* series. However, it is the second book in chronological order. Mr. Lewis dedicated this book to Lucy Barfield, who was the daughter of his close friend Owen Barfield. *The Lion, the Witch and the Wardrobe* was published in 1950 by Geoffrey Bles. Here is a brief synopsis of it:

During World War II, the four Pevensie children, Peter, Susan, Edmund, and Lucy, have to be sent away from their home in London because the Nazi Germans are bombing the city. They go to live in the house of Professor Digory Kirke, who lives in the country.

One day, while they are exploring his house, they discover a wardrobe in a spare room. Lucy goes inside the wardrobe and is transported to the magical land of Narnia. She walks through the woods, finds a lamp-post, and meets Mr. Tumnus the faun. During her visit with him, she learns about the evil White Witch Jadis, who calls herself the Queen of Narnia. (This is the same Jadis from *The Magician's Nephew.*) Jadis has cast an evil spell on Narnia that has made it always winter, but never Christmas.

Eventually, Edmund also reaches Narnia through the wardrobe, and he meets the evil White Witch. She tells him that she will make him a Prince of Narnia if he will simply go home and bring his brother and sisters back to her. Edmund, a selfish and ignorant boy, agrees to the witch's plan and tries to bring his siblings to her.

After a series of events, all four of the children end up in Narnia together, and they meet Mr. and Mrs. Beaver. The Beavers tell the children that they are part of a prophecy that says when four human beings become the rulers of Narnia, the reign of the White Witch will end. During their conversation, Edmund sneaks off to the witch's castle, where he is taken prisoner. The Beavers then bring Peter, Susan, and Lucy to the great lion Aslan for help. Aslan has gathered an army of Narnians at the Stone Table to fight the White Witch.

Edmund is rescued, and afterwards, the witch demands that he be killed for his treachery to his family. Instead, Aslan sacrifices himself and dies in Edmund's place. After he has been killed on the Stone Table, Aslan rises from the dead and comes back to life. By doing this, he breaks the witch's evil spell on Narnia.

Peter leads the Narnians to fight against the army of the White Witch. The Narnians win the battle, and Aslan kills the witch. Peter, Susan, Edmund, and Lucy are then crowned Kings and Queens of Narnia at the castle Cair Paravel.

One day, many years later (in Narnian time), the siblings are hunting in the woods when they stumble upon the lamp-post and accidentally return to their own world (Earth). However, because time is different in Narnia, only a few seconds have passed in their world since the time they entered the wardrobe together.

The Lamp-post by L.B. Dugan

Shasta and Bree *by L.B. Dugan*

C.S. Lewis finished writing *The Horse and His Boy* by July of 1950. It was the fourth book written in *The Chronicles of Narnia* series but is the third book in chronological order. Mr. Lewis dedicated this book to David and Douglas Gresham, who were the sons of his (future) wife, Joy Davidman (see Chapter 7: "Marriage and Last Years"). *The Horse and His Boy* was published in 1954 by Geoffrey Bles. Here is a brief synopsis of it:

Shasta is a poor boy living in Calormen, which is a land south of Narnia. He runs away from his home to avoid being sold as a slave. Along the way, he meets the Talking Horse Bree from Narnia, who had been forced into slavery in Calormen. The two of them agree to escape together to the North. On their journey, they meet a girl named Aravis and her Talking Horse Hwin, who was also taken captive from Narnia. Aravis is a Calormene noblewoman, and she has run away from home because her father was going to force her to marry an evil leader named Ahoshta Tarkaan.

Shasta, Bree, Aravis, and Hwin make it to Tashbaan, the capital city of Calormen, where the ruler of the land lives. During this time, Peter, Edmund, Susan, and Lucy are ruling Narnia. King Edmund and Queen Susan happen to be visiting Tashbaan when the runaways arrive.

Shasta looks just like Prince Corin of Archenland, who is also visiting the city with King Edmund and Queen Susan. Someone mistakes Shasta for Prince Corin, and he is taken to the palace in Tashbaan.

When Shasta arrives at the palace, he meets the real prince, who helps him escape so he can continue on his journey. Meanwhile, Aravis overhears a conversation between the ruler of Calormen and his son, Prince

Rabadash, who are discussing plans to attack Archenland and Narnia. Shasta, Aravis, Bree, and Hwin escape from Tashbaan and travel north to warn King Lune of Archenland about Prince Rabadash's plans.

While Shasta and his companions are on their way to Archenland, a lion begins to follow them. They later discover that it is the great lion Aslan. Eventually, they make it to Archenland and find shelter with the Hermit of the Southern March. Shasta decides to leave and go alone to warn King Lune of the coming attack. Along the way, he meets Aslan and realizes that he is lord of all creation and is worthy of honor and glory.

After his encounter with Aslan, Shasta sees King Lune in the woods and tells him about the planned attack. The King prepares to defend his castle, Anvard, and soon after, an army from Narnia arrives to help him fight. When Prince Rabadash and his army reach the castle, a great battle begins. The Calormenes are defeated, and Aravis, Bree, and Hwin return to celebrate the victory.

After the battle, it is discovered that Shasta is the long-lost brother of Prince Corin and that his real name is Cor. He is reunited with his father, King Lune, and eventually becomes King Cor of Archenland and marries his close friend Aravis.

The City of Tashbaan *by L.B. Dugan*

13 Prince Caspian: A Synopsis (1951)

Prince Caspian Fleeing Miraz *by L.B. Dugan*

C.S. Lewis finished writing *Prince Caspian: The Return to Narnia* by December of 1949. It was the second book written in *The Chronicles of Narnia* series but is the fourth book in chronological order. Interestingly, *Prince Caspian* is the only Narnia book with a subtitle. Mr. Lewis dedicated this book to Mary Clare Havard, who was the daughter of his friend Dr. Robert E. Havard. *Prince Caspian* was published in 1951 by Geoffrey Bles. Here is a brief synopsis of it:

It has been one year since the four Pevensie children, Peter, Susan, Edmund, and Lucy, have returned home from Narnia. One day, while they are waiting at a train station, they are suddenly brought back to Narnia. They discover that their castle, Cair Paravel, is now destroyed and in ruins.

They meet Trumpkin the Dwarf, who tells them what has happened since they left (it has actually been hundreds of years in Narnian time): Many years ago, men from the land of Telmar invaded Narnia and took over the land. One of the Telmarine Kings was Caspian the Ninth. Caspian's brother, Miraz, was jealous and wanted the throne for himself.

In order to become King, Miraz killed his brother Caspian and eventually tried to kill Caspian's son, Caspian the Tenth. On the night that Miraz's wife gave birth to a son, Prince Caspian the Tenth escaped from his evil uncle with the help of his tutor, Doctor Cornelius. For many years, Doctor Cornelius had been telling Caspian tales of what Narnia was like before the Telmarines invaded. Miraz had actually forbidden those stories from being told because he wanted all of the Narnians to be destroyed and forgotten forever.

Prince Caspian escaped into the woods and encountered some Narnians, who agreed to help him fight for the Telmarine throne. Because he knew that a battle was coming, Prince Caspian blew Susan's horn, which the Narnians believed could bring them help when they needed it. (This is how the four Pevensie children were suddenly brought back to Narnia from the train station.)

After he finishes telling the four children about Prince Caspian, Trumpkin the Dwarf takes them to Aslan's How, where Caspian has gathered his army. (Aslan's How is a large green mound of earth that was built overtop of the ancient Stone Table.) On the way there, Trumpkin and the children meet Aslan, and he begins to gather all the Narnians who are still faithful to him.

Meanwhile, Miraz and his Telmarine army have arrived at Aslan's How to fight the Narnians. Peter is there and challenges Miraz to a fight. Near the end of the fight, two of Miraz's soldiers betray and kill him. However, they try to blame the Narnians for his death in hopes of starting a war. A great battle occurs, and the Telmarines are defeated. Caspian is then crowned King of Narnia, and peace is brought back to the land. Aslan tells Peter and Susan that this is their last adventure in Narnia and that they will not be returning. He then sends the four Pevensie children back to their own world.

Aslan's How *by L.B. Dugan*

The *Dawn Treader* by L.B. Dugan

C.S. Lewis finished writing *The Voyage of the Dawn Treader* by February of 1950. It was the third book written in *The Chronicles of Narnia* series but is the fifth book in chronological order. Mr. Lewis dedicated this book to Geoffrey Barfield, who was the son of his good friend Owen Barfield. *The Voyage of the Dawn Treader* was published in 1952 by Geoffrey Bles. Here is a brief synopsis of it:

Edmund and Lucy Pevensie have been sent to live with their Aunt Alberta, Uncle Harold, and cousin Eustace in Cambridge, England. Eustace Clarence Scrubb is a miserable boy who believes fairy tales are nonsense.

One day, Edmund, Lucy, and Eustace are brought into Narnia through a picture on the wall in Lucy's bedroom. They land in the sea and are rescued by men from the Narnian ship *Dawn Treader*. They are greeted by King Caspian the Tenth, who was once Prince Caspian. They also see their old friend Reepicheep, a brave talking mouse, who is sailing with the crew. Caspian tells them that he is on a voyage to find seven missing Telmarine lords. Many years ago, these lords had been sent off to sea by his wicked uncle, Miraz, because they supported the true King, Caspian the Ninth. Miraz had hoped that they would die at sea and never return.

Meanwhile, Eustace is giving everyone on board a hard time and is complaining about everything. Eventually, the *Dawn Treader* arrives at an island, and when the crew goes ashore, Eustace leaves without telling anyone. He finds a large treasure hoard and is magically turned into a dragon as a punishment for his greed. Eustace realizes that he has been acting wrongly and humbles himself. The great lion Aslan then turns him back into a boy, and he is no longer the snob that Edmund and Lucy remember.

After these events, the crew of the *Dawn Treader* continue their voyage at sea. They come to an island where they meet invisible Monopods, who have only one foot. Lucy goes to the Magician's House on the island and reads a spell from the Magic Book, which makes the Monopods visible again. The Magician of the island gives the crew of the *Dawn Treader* advice for their voyage.

Soon after leaving the island, they pass a place called Dark Island, and they can feel the presence of evil. While they are near Dark Island, they save Lord Rhoop, one of the seven Telmarine lords they had been looking for. He had been tormented by the dark power of the island.

King Caspian and his crew soon reach the beginning of the End of the World, which is close to Aslan's country. They arrive on another island and find the last three Telmarine lords, who are under a magical spell. (They had found the first four lords earlier in their voyage). While there, they meet Ramandu, who was once a star, and he gives them advice for the final part of their journey.

At last, they reach the End of the World, and Edmund, Lucy, Eustace, and Reepicheep travel alone to the shores of Aslan's country. Reepicheep happily sails on to the country he has been looking forward to his whole life, and Aslan sends Edmund, Lucy, and Eustace back to their world.

The Shores of Aslan's Country *by L.B. Dugan*

15 The Silver Chair: A Synopsis (1953)

Puddleglum the Marsh-wiggle *by L.B. Dugan*

C.S. Lewis finished writing *The Silver Chair* by March of 1951. It was the fifth book written in *The Chronicles of Narnia* series but is the sixth book in chronological order. Mr. Lewis dedicated this book to Nicholas Hardie, who was the son of his friend Colin Hardie. *The Silver Chair* was published in 1953 by Geoffrey Bles. Here is a brief synopsis of it:

Eustace Scrubb and his friend Jill Pole are students at a horrible school called Experiment House. It has only been a few months since Eustace was brought to Narnia (see Chapter 14: "*The Voyage of the Dawn Treader: A Symopsis*"). One day, Eustace and Jill are magically brought to the Mountain of Aslan, where Jill first meets the great lion Aslan. He tells her that their mission in Narnia is to find Prince Rilian, son of King Caspian the Tenth. Prince Rilian was lost many years ago because of an evil witch, and King Caspian has given up hope of ever finding his son.

After Aslan sends them to Narnia, Eustace and Jill arrive at the castle Cair Paravel and see Trumpkin the Dwarf, who is now very old. In order to help them continue their journey, the owl Glimfeather brings them to the land of the Marsh-wiggles, who live north of Cair Paravel. The gloomy Marsh-wiggle Puddleglum agrees to accompany the two children on their quest to find Prince Rilian. They travel across the northern lands and meet the Lady of the Green Kirtle, who directs them to Harfang Castle, home of the giants.

When they arrive at Harfang Castle, they are greeted by the giants, who secretly want to eat them. The three travelers realize that the way to find Prince Rilian is to go underground beneath the City Ruinous, which is near the castle. They eventually escape from the giants and run to the City Ruinous.

Eustace, Jill, and Puddleglum discover Underland, where they meet the Earthmen, who are servants of a terrible witch. The Earthmen take the three of them to the house of the witch, where they meet a black knight. They discover that this knight is Prince Rilian in disguise, and they break the silver chair, which is what the witch used to keep him under a powerful spell.

The witch arrives and begins to cast a spell on the four of them. She tries to trick them into believing that all they have ever known, including the sun, the earth above, and even Aslan himself, are all fake. Puddleglum bravely stands up to the witch and breaks her spell. However, she turns herself into a green serpent and attacks them, but she gets killed by Prince Rilian.

The prince then leads Eustace, Jill, and Puddleglum out of Underland and into Narnia. They arrive back at Cair Paravel just in time for Prince Rilian to see his father, King Caspian, before he dies. Eustace and Jill are taken to the Mountain of Aslan, where they see Aslan again. While they are there, Aslan brings King Caspian back to life on the mountain, and he becomes young again. Aslan then allows Caspian to return with Eustace and Jill for a short time to their school Experiment House to teach the bullies there a good lesson. Afterwards, Caspian and Aslan say goodbye to Eustace and Jill, who have become great friends while on their adventure in Narnia.

The Silver Chair *by Solomon Schmidt*

16 The Last Battle: A Synopsis (1956)

Shift Dresses Puzzle in a Lion Skin *by L.B. Dugan*

C.S. Lewis finished writing *The Last Battle* by May of 1953. It was the sixth book written in *The Chronicles of Narnia* series but is the seventh book in chronological order. Interestingly, it is the only Narnia book that Mr. Lewis did not dedicate to anyone. *The Last Battle* was published in 1956 by Geoffrey Bles. Here is a brief synopsis of it:

Two hundred years have passed in Narnia since the great lion Aslan has been seen by anyone. Shift the Ape forms a plan to trick the Narnians into obeying his orders. He dresses a clueless donkey named Puzzle in a lion skin and tells the creatures of Narnia that it is Aslan. The trickery works, and Shift uses Puzzle to rule over the Narnians. During this time of deceit, men from the land of Calormen invade Narnia and take its King, Tirian, as their prisoner.

Shift the Ape gathers the Narnians on Stable Hill, and makes Puzzle come out and pretend to be Aslan. The fooled Narnians listen to Shift and believe that he is telling them Aslan's commands. The Calormenes also come to Stable Hill and use Shift to give orders to the Narnians so that they can control them.

King Tirian, who is still being held by the Calormenes, calls for help. In answer to his cry, Eustace Scrubb and Jill Pole are brought back to Narnia to help rescue the King. When they arrive, they free King Tirian and escape from Stable Hill, along with Jewel the Unicorn. They also secretly take Puzzle the donkey with them.

While the five of them are traveling along, they encounter Tash, a terrible demon from Calormen, who is on his way to Stable Hill. They also receive terrible news from Farsight the Eagle that King Tirian's castle, Cair Paravel, has been attacked and taken over by the

Calormenes. King Tirian and his friends decide that the only way to free the Narnians is to show them that Shift the Ape has been tricking them all this time. They return to Stable Hill, and King Tirian throws Shift into the stable. Tash, the demon, has been waiting inside and devours him.

After this, the last battle in Narnian history takes place in front of the stable. King Tirian, his friends, and the loyal Narnians fight against the Calormene soldiers. During the battle, King Tirian is forced inside the stable, where he meets the true Aslan. Meanwhile, Tash, the demon from Calormen, is banished from the world into his own evil realm forever.

King Tirian finds himself in a wide open country and meets many of the kings and queens of Narnia from the past. He also sees his friends Eustace and Jill, who had helped him fight in the Last Battle.

Aslan then begins the Last Judgment of Narnia. The faithful Narnians enter inside the Stable Door, and the world outside is destroyed. Aslan brings all of them to the Garden of Paradise, which is the heart of Aslan's country. Here the Narnians are reunited with Reepicheep, the mouse, and many others. Aslan tells Jill and Eustace that they have actually died in their own world and are now in his country to live forever.

Shift Presenting "Aslan" to the Narnians on Stable Hill *by L.B. Dugan*

Congratulations! You have finished reading *The Life & Works of C.S. Lewis History Bites.*

I hope you have enjoyed it and will continue to learn more about C.S. Lewis and his writings.

~Solomon

GLOSSARY

A

Academic year – this was the time from October to early July while C.S. Lewis was at Oxford University

Aired – played or broadcast on television or radio

Apologist – someone who defends his/her religion through books and speeches

Army reserve – a group of soldiers ready to fight when called to active duty

Autobiography – a book that someone writes about his/her own life

B

Basis – the primary idea behind a book

Blunt – to the point or very direct

Corresponding – writing back and forth

Demobilized – released from the military

District – an area of land in a city

Fellowship – the rank of a fellow at a college

Financially – having to do with money

Flying colors – passing a test easily with a very good grade

Handyman – a person who is hired to fix things around a house

Headmaster – the person in charge of a private school

Literary critic – someone who studies and writes about works of literature

Literature – a collection of writings that have great value and importance

Logical – thinking through something clearly

Manuscript – a copy of a book that is written by hand and has not been published yet

Philosophy – the study of knowledge

Pub – a bar or tavern that serves food and drinks

Refugee – a person who has to leave his/her home in order to escape danger

Regiment – a unit of soldiers in the military that is usually made up of two battalions

Registry office – a place in Great Britain where people get married and where birth and death records are kept

Regress – going back to something

Reluctant – hesitant to make a decision

Scholarship – a gift of money to attend a college or university

Solicitor – a type of lawyer in Great Britain who represents people in the lower courts

Theist – someone who believes in the existence of God

Tutored – taught privately about a particular subject

Visa – permission from the government to enter and live in a country for a limited time